10 Chapters to Having a Successful Investment Portfolio

Martin Krikorian

iUniverse, Inc.
New York   Bloomington

10 Chapters to Having a Successful Investment Portfolio

The information, ideas, and suggestions in this book are not intended to render professional advice. Before following any suggestions contained in this book, you should consult your personal accountant or other financial advisor. Neither the author nor the publisher shall be liable or responsible for any loss or damage allegedly arising as a consequence of your use or application of any information or suggestions in this book.

iUniverse books may be ordered through booksellers or by contacting:

iUniverse
1663 Liberty Drive
Bloomington, IN 47403
www.iuniverse.com
1-800-Authors (1-800-288-4677)

Because of the dynamic nature of the Internet, any Web addresses or links contained in this book may have changed since publication and may no longer be valid. The views expressed in this work are solely those of the author and do not necessarily reflect the views of the publisher, and the publisher hereby disclaims any responsibility for them.

ISBN: 978-0-595-48613-7 (pbk)
ISBN: 978-0-595-48993-0 (cloth)
ISBN: 978-0-595-60707-5 (ebk)

Printed in the United States of America

Contents

Chapter 1
Tuning Out the Fortune-Tellers

Every January the fortune-tellers come out and make their predictions about the stock market for the upcoming year. As a result, investors will turn to the financial media, most notably CNBC, hoping to gain some insight on the future movement of the market and stocks within it. The stock analysts interviewed by Maria Bartoromo and company will provide information that sounds so convincing that many will be willing to bet some, if not most, of their retirement savings on the predictions.

The so-called market experts on CNBC can ramble on all they want about historical trends, moving averages, the Fed, and other factors that will drive the stock market one way or the other. The truth is, they don't know any more than you do about where the market will go. Do you honestly think the folks at CNBC actually take the predictions of these gurus seriously? Of course not. However, to keep you watching, CNBC knows they must pander to the part of you that wants to believe these gurus are letting you in on the inside track to getting rich. Unfortunately, investors give the predictions of these false prophets and this shameless bunch of stock touts far more weight than they should.

Nevertheless, hope springs eternal. Because people want to believe there are experts who hold the Holy Grail to future returns, there's no shortage of self-anointed fortune-tellers making predictions these days. Unfortunately, there is a shortage of accountability when it comes to their predictions. Individuals who are either arrogant enough, or naïve enough, to think they can consistently predict the direction of the market or the individual stocks within it should be held accountable for those predictions. Rather than simply making a prediction, they should also provide a confidence level figure for each of their predictions. For example:

Prediction:	**Confidence Level:**
"The Dow Jones will end the year between 12,000 and 12,500"	90%
"XYZ stock will earn between 15 and 17 percent this year"	75%
"The ABC mutual fund will outperform the S&P 500 index this year"	80%

If it were possible to make reliable predictions about when the market will rise or fall, the market would respond in advance, and it could not then rise and fall in the way it does. During any investment period there will always be a certain number of unforseeable economic and political events such as natural disasters, political turmoil, terrorist attacks, to name just a few, that will affect the market. These unforeseeable circumstances provide the fortune-tellers with their defense for missing their original "can't-miss" predictions. If the fortune-tellers held themselves accountable, it wouldn't take the investing public long to realize that they are just as likely to get as good a prediction about the stock market by calling one of those 900 psychic hotline numbers.

The truth is that no one—not you, me, the pundits from the big brokerage firms, the newsletter writers, your broker, or financial advisor—can predict what the market will do. Even the world's greatest investor can't predict the future. When asked about his opinion on the direction of the stock market, Warren Buffet once stated, "I never have the faintest idea what the stock market is going to do in the next six months, or the next year, or the next two."

If there is one thing I have learned after thirteen years in the invesment industry, it is that there are three kinds of investors and investment professionals:

1. Those who don't know where the market is headed
2. Those who don't know that they don't know where the market is headed
3. Those who don't know where the market is headed but get paid a lot of money to pretend that they do.

Notes

Notes

Chapter 2
Playing the Loser's Game

Individual Stocks

The popular investment phrase "a rising tide lifts all boats" was never more evident than during the bull market of the late 1990's. It seemed that no matter what stocks you invested in, you couldn't help but make money. After all, who could forget the commercial in which a suburban mom, who's returning home from jogging, punches a few keys on her computer, sells a little biotech stock, and announces, "I think I just made about $1,700." What about the ad for an online trading brokerage firm in which a tow-truck driver, and his passenger, have the following conversation.

> Passenger: You invest online?
> Tow-truck driver: Oh yea, big time. Well, last few years anyway. I'm retired now.
> Passenger: You're retired?
> Driver: I don't need to do *this*—I just like helping people.
> Passenger: (Noticing a picture of an island) Vacation spot?
> Driver: Actually, it's a picture of my house.
> Passenger: It's an island.

Driver: Well, technically it's a country. Weird thing about owning your own country, though, you have to name it.

Obviously, the gains achieved by the characters in these ads were fictional. Unfortunately, for the thousands of investors who lost a small fortune during the stock trading frenzy during the late 1990s, their losses were not.

It never ceases to amaze me that most investors think that by paying a couple of hundred dollars for a newsletter, by logging onto Yahoo!, or by relying on the stock predictions of their favorite financial publications they can consistently pick stocks that will outperform the market. Unfortunately, this type information provides you with no more ability to pick individual stocks than to pick numbers on a roulette wheel.

Imagine you just finished reading an article in the *Wall Street Journal* about the XYZ Companies new product line that could revolutionize its industry. Its stock is currently selling at $50, and after reading the article, you are quite confident that its share price will go to $75 or possibly even $100, so you decide to buy it. Now think where you just read this new, insightful information, in one of the most popular financial newspapers in the country. The truth is, if you read about XYZ in the *Wall Street Journal*, the chances are pretty good that thousands of other investors read the same article. What about the hundred or so stock analysts covering XYZ for billion-dollar pension firms and mutual fund companies? Do you really think they would let a stock that is obviously worth $75 or $100, sit there at $50 without rushing out to buy it? The reason XYZ is trading at $50 is that the information available publicly about the stock has already been factored into its price. As a result, the market as a whole thinks that it is worth $50 and not $75 or $100.

With so much investing information available today via the Internet, financial publications, investment newsletters, and cable television, finding information about a company is easy. Finding "useful information," however, that has not already been factored into the price of its stock is not. Confusing the two is perhaps the most common misperception individuals have about investing in individual stocks. There are basically two ways individual stock investors can consistently outperform the market. The first is by having privileged insider information about a company. To trade on such information however, is a violation of the securities laws of the United States (just ask Martha Stewart). The second way is to interpret the information differently (and more correctly) from the way in which the market collectively does. In other words, to outperform the market, you must consistently discover and exploit investment opportunities that have been missed by other investors due to their errors, incompetence, and/or inattention.

Unfortunately, over the last few years thousands of investors learned the hard way about the risk of investing in individual stocks. Many investors were outraged when Enron, the seventh largest company in the United States, lost tens of billions of dollars and went into bankruptcy in 2001. I can certainly sympathize with individuals who sustained these significant losses, but part of the risk of investing in individual stocks has always been that you might end up holding an Enron. Every year some companies, no matter how much you think you may know about them, are going to fail, whether it's due to greed, incompetence, a corrupt CEO, or bad luck. But the cause of the failure is irrelevant to you as the investor; your money is still just as lost. What should matter to you is developing an alternative approach to investing that can help protect your savings from this kind of risk. There is an alternative, mutual funds.

The majority of mutual funds typically own hundreds of different stocks in many different industries. As we have seen in the past, corporate bankruptcies (Enron, WorldCom, and Global Crossing, just to name a few) can wipe away an investor's hard-earned money. However, holding a properly diversified portfolio of mutual funds can help insulate investors from the adverse market events that can negatively affect a company, country, region, or asset class.

If you are smarter, have better insight, and have access to more useful investing information than the rest of the market, you should probably continue investing in individual stocks. However, for those of you who are less confident in your ability to predict the future, you may want to consider investing in mutual funds.

Chasing "Hot" Funds

In addition to the gurus on television, the personal financial magazines also provide their favorite and top-performing mutual funds lists for the New Year. With all the subtlety of a thirty-minute late-night infomercial, they each find some way to rank the funds on performance and risk, and crown their selections as "the best." And every January millions of people read these magazines, look at these lists of top-performing funds over the last year, and think, "Wow, those are the funds I need to be in this year!"

According to the Investment Company Institute, 88 percent of investors cite past performance as the primary reason they select one fund over another. After all, it seems perfectly reasonable to think that if a fund posted an above-average return in one year, it's got a pretty good shot of doing it again next year too. However, just because a fund produced a year of above-average performance does not mean that one should expect above-average performance the following year.

To those 88 percent of investors, I would like to offer my suggestion on how you can better use these guides to select your mutual funds. Crumple them up, and throw them in the trash. These lists are like reporting the recent winning numbers on a roulette wheel—they indicate little or nothing about what is likely to happen on the next roll. If picking mutual funds were as simple as buying those funds with the best recent performance, accumulating wealth would be a cinch. The problem is that the latest list-topping, "hot" mutual funds rarely manage to stay among the top performers. Every year, we see entirely new mutual funds at the top of the lists. In fact, many of the top-ten funds in one year end up in the bottom quartile the next.

Industry studies have demonstrated that utilizing the past performance of a mutual fund is a poor predictor of its future performance. To illustrate this phenomenon, the chart below shows the top-performing mutual funds from 2001 through 2005 along with their performance the following year.

If past performance had predictive value, the top funds should repeat year after year. However, as the following chart demonstrates, top-performing funds don't repeat each year. The question investors need to ask themselves is: if the same funds don't repeat, just how valuable are these lists?

Fund Rank 2001	2002	Fund Rank 2002	2003	Fund Rank 2003	2004	Fund Rank 2004	2005	Fund Rank 2005	2006
1	35	1	1,067	1	5,989	1	250	1	2,337
2	945	2	509	2	6,045	2	1,402	2	7
3	4,515	3	714	3	139	3	2,062	3	2,813
4	2,849	4	467	4	5,954	4	75	4	994
5	3,384	5	20	5	1,009	5	54	5	6,273
6	3,126	6	826	6	70	6	305	6	15
7	1,392	7	106	7	5,450	7	33	7	156
8	1,741	8	587	8	223	8	9	8	2,610
9	1,579	9	127	9	2,893	9	560	9	4,695
10	2,874	10	87	10	1,467	10	29	10	53

Source: Morningstar Principia

If past performance, ranking systems, and other methods do not work in selecting mutual funds, what does? The single factor that best explains why some funds end up on the top-performing lists and some don't is not the result of superior fund management, but rather the result of a hot sector, or asset class. Almost any fund devoted to a recent hot sector is going to do well, regardless of the talents of its fund manager. The most brilliant manager of a large-cap growth fund will under perform an average manager of a small-cap value fund in years when cap small cap value stocks are the top-performing asset class.

The financial media performs a valuable service when they provide the investing public with investment information to make better investing decisions. Unfortunately, that's more the exception than the rule. And "top ten" mutual fund lists are one of the most useless lists of information they provide the investing public with.

Timing the Market

Most investors try to "time" the market, i.e., they attempt to buy stocks when they think the market is going to go up and attempt to sell stocks when they expect the market to fall. In order to work successfully, this approach requires either accurate predictive abilities or access to someone who possesses those abilities.

For example if you invested $100,000 in the S&P 500˚ Index on December 31, 1995, by December 31, 2005, your $100,000 would have grown to $239,040, for an average annual total return of 9.11 percent. Suppose you decided to get out of the market, and as a result missed the market's ten best single-day performances. In that case, your 9.11 percent return would have fallen to 4.06 percent. If you had missed the market's twenty best days, that 9.11 percent return would have dropped to 0.25 percent. If you had missed the market's forty best days, that 9.11 percent return would have turned into a loss of 5.75 percent. In other words, by missing the forty best days, your retirement savings when have gone from being worth $239,040, to only $33,570.

Period of Investment	Average Annual Total Return	Growth of $100,000
Fully Invested (2,516 days)	9.11%	$239,040
Miss the 10 Best Days	4.06	148,930
Miss the 20 Best Days	0.25	102,570
Miss the 30 Best Days	-3.02	73,570
Miss the 40 Best Days	-5.75	55,310

Source: Fact Set Research Systems Inc. The S&P 500 Index is an unmanaged index considered representative of the U.S. stock market. Performance reflects reinvestment of dividends

There is no question that if you can get into the market just before a big rally, you will do very well. The problem is that stock market rallies often occur in brief and unexpected periods of time. The following four charts illustrate just how concentrated stock market rallies can be.

The stock market's profit for 2006 occurred in an eighteen-week period from July 20 to December 5

2006	
Jan 1 - Jul 19	0%
Jul 20 - Dec 5	15.6%
Dec 6 - Dec 31	0%
Annual Return	**15.6%**

In 2004 the stock market's profit occurred in the last seven weeks of the year

2004	
Jan 1 – Nov 7	0%
Nov 8 – Dec 31	10.7%
Annual Return	**10.7%**

In 1998 the entire year's profit was earned in the last eleven weeks of the year

1997	
Jan 1 – Apr 14	0%
Apr 15 - Aug 6	33.4%
Aug 7 – Dec 31	0%
Annual Return	**33.4%**

In 1997 the entire year's profit was in the middle fifteen weeks of the year

1998	
Jan 1 – Oct 7	0%
Oct 8 – Dec 31	28.6%
Annual Return	**28.6%**

Stock market represented by the S&P 500 Index. Source: Ibbotson Associates

Whether it's market timing or chasing after hot stocks and top-performing mutual funds, the evidence is pretty overwhelming that none of these things does anything but lose you money. Yet, consciously or unconsciously, this is what most people do. The sad truth is, most investors do not know that what they are doing amounts to gambling with their retirement savings. As you can see, this is not only my opinion, but it is also the opinion of some of the most brilliant minds in the investment industry.

Here are some examples:

> "I never have the faintest idea what the stock market is going to do in the next six months, or the next year, or the next two." *Warren Buffet, CEO of Berkshire Hathaway*

> "If I have noticed anything over these 60 years on Wall Street, it is that people do not succeed in

forecasting what's going to happen to the stock market." *Benjamin Graham, legendary investor and co-author of the 1934 classic, Security Analysis*

"The market timer's Hall of Fame is an empty room." *Jane Bryant Quinn, syndicated columnist and author of Smart and Simple Financial Strategies for Busy People*

"There will always be someone predicting disaster and someone predicting great fortune. At one time or another, each will be closer to correct than the other. But it won't matter to you if you understand this and have invested responsibly. You have a long-term plan; stick with it." *Peter Lynch, Former Fidelity fund manager of Magellan Fund*

"Market Timing is a poor substitute for a long-term investment plan." *Jonathan Clements, journalist, Wall Street Journal*

"I've been around this business darn near a half-century, and I know I can't do it successfully. In fact, I don't even know anyone who knows anyone who has ever successfully timed the market over the long term." *Jack Bogle, Founder and Chairman of The Vanguard Group*

"There is an overwhelming body of evidence to support the view that believing in the ability of market timers is the equivalent of believing astrologers can predict the future." *Larry Swedroe, author of What Wall Street Doesn't Want You to Know*

"If we haven't said it enough, we'll say it again: Market timing is dangerous." *Barron's Guide to Making Investment Decisions*

Notes

Notes

Chapter 3
Diversification

What Diversification Isn't

Many investors assume that by owning a bunch of mutual funds with different names, from different fund families, they are diversified. However, simply owning a large number of mutual funds is not diversification. There is no benefit gained by investing in mutual funds that have a consistently high positive correlation to one another. During the late 1990s, many individuals thought they were diversifying their portfolios by purchasing several different growth mutual funds; however, most of those funds were heavily weighted in the same group of technology and communications stocks. The following chart illustrates the returns of two popular mutual funds during the bull market of the late 1990s and the bear market from 2000-2002. The mutual funds provided above-average returns from 1997-1999, however owning both funds did nothing to reduce risk during the bear market of 2000-2002. When the technology and communications sectors of the economy "tanked" during this period their 401k savings tanked as well.

A Poorly Diversified Portfolio

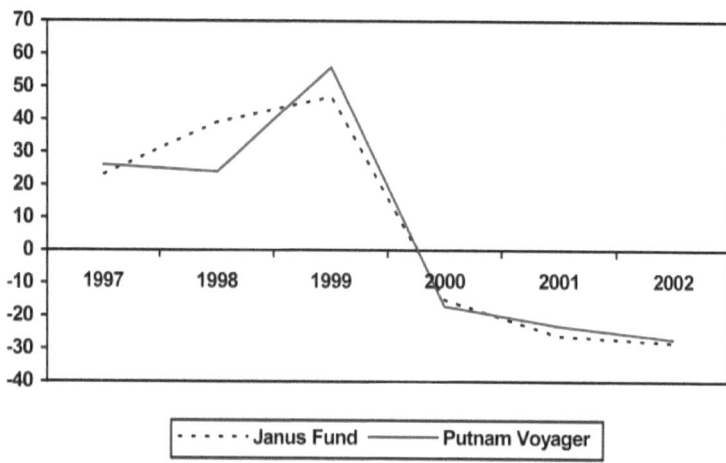

When it comes to choosing which mutual funds to include in one's retirement portfolio, most people make the mistake of choosing mutual funds based solely on their individual performance, rather than on how the performance of each fund will affect the overall performance of their portfolio.

How Diversification Works

You hear it so often. When it comes to managing your investments, you need to diversify. But what does diversification exactly mean? The following example may shed some light.

Imagine there is an island economy with two companies. One sells sunglasses, and one sells umbrellas. (See chart). You have two thousand dollars to invest, and you would like to earn 10 percent on your money, but you are not sure which company to invest in. You know that during sunny seasons the company selling sunglasses does a booming business, and you know that umbrellas sales plunge. During rainy seasons, the company selling sunglasses loses money, and umbrella sales soar. What you don't know is what the weather will do in the future. On average, half of the seasons should be sunny and half rainy, so investing in either company should provide you with an average return of 10 percent. However, there is always a chance that there could be several rainy or sunny seasons in a row, so if you guess wrong you could potentially lose money. So, which company is the better investment? Suppose that instead of investing the entire $2,000 in one company, you invest $1,000 (half) in both companies.

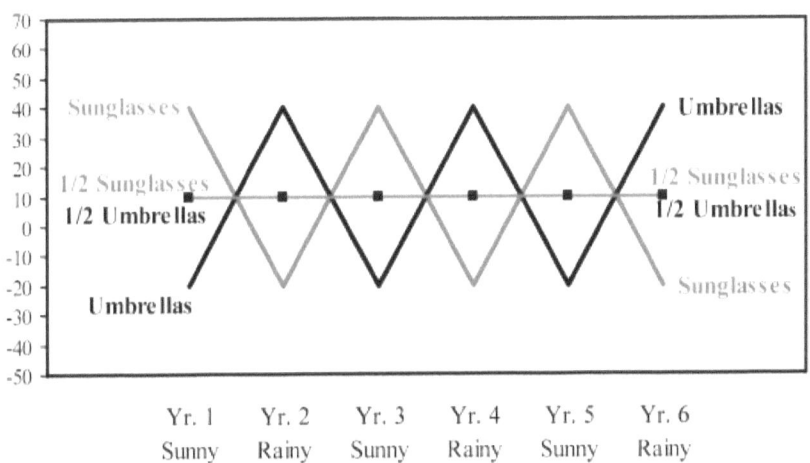

The chart above shows that during the three sunny seasons, the company selling sunglasses gains 40 percent, and the company selling umbrellas loses 20 percent. The diversified portfolio invested in both companies earned 10 percent all three years. During the three rainy seasons, the company selling umbrellas now gains 40 percent while the company selling sunglasses loses 20 percent. The diversified portfolio, however, once again earns 10 percent in all three years. During the six-year period, the diversified portfolio returned 10 percent every year, *no matter what the weather did.*

Are You Guessing or Diversifying?

When it comes to investing, one of the most common mistakes occurs when investors decide to buy an investment in an asset class that has done well in the recent past and to sell an asset class that has done poorly. Unfortunately, such a strategy over time results in poor performance. Just how poor?

A study based on mutual fund money flows by Dalbar Research, a Boston investment research firm, found that for the twenty years 1986–2005, the S&P 500® index had an annualized return of 11.9 percent, while the average equity fund investor had significantly lower returns—only 3.9 percent annualized (barely staying ahead of inflation at 3 percent). The problem is that market cycles have proven to be inherently unpredictable, making it next to impossible to be consistently successful at timing the market. The following chart shows how four equity asset classes have done individually over the last twenty years. The first two asset classes are U.S. large- and U.S. small-cap stocks, the next two are international large and international small stocks. The last column is an annually rebalanced diversified portfolio consisting of all four assets. Based on these past returns, can you say with confidence which asset class will be the best performer next year? If you had to invest all of your retirement savings in one investment, each year, over the next twenty years, which would you choose?

	U.S. Large	U.S. Small	Int'l Large	Int'l Small	25% Each
1987		Worst		Best	
1988	Worst		Best		
1989	Best		Worst		
1990	Best		Worst		
1991		Best		Worst	
1992		Best		Worst	
1993	Worst			Best	
1994		Worst		Best	
1995	Best			Worst	
1996	Best			Worst	
1997	Best			Worst	
1998	Best	Worst			
1999		Worst	Best		
2000		Best	Worst		
2001		Best	Worst		
2002	Worst			Best	
2003	Worst			Best	
2004	Worst			Best	
2005		Worst		Best	
2006	Worst		Best		
# Best Yrs	6	4	3	7	**0**
# Worst Yrs	6	5	4	5	**0**
Avg. Return	11.8	12.8	9.7	12.1	**12.3**

Sources: Standard & Poor's 500 Composite Index (U.S. large-company stocks), Russell 200 Index; (U.S. small-company stocks); MSCI EAFE ® (Europe, Australia, Far East) Index (international stocks); IFA International Small Company Index (International small company stocks)

Since different classes and styles of investments move up and down in value at different times, combining them in a diversified portfolio can produce more stable returns. Notice on the chart that by moving all the way to right, an investor who chose the portfolio diversified among each of the four asset classes was never the best or worst performing investment in any of the 20 years, yet it still managed to outperform three of the four asset classes.

When it comes to saving for retirement, we could all build a perfect portfolio if we knew in advance which investments will perform well in the future, and which ones will not. Unfortunately, asset classes don't go up or down in a straight line any more than .300 hitters in baseball get three hits in every ten at bats. Just as there is no way to predict when a hitter will either go into a slump or go on a hot streak, we cannot predict when any particular asset class will be a winner or a loser. The top-performing asset class in one year is just as likely to repeat as fall to the bottom. In some years, small companies are best performers, and in some years they are the worst. In other years, large companies may rise to the top. This cyclical nature of the market often makes it tempting for investors to try to guess which asset class or asset style will be the next hot investment.

Yet, despite an overwhelming amount of evidence that has demonstrated that market timing is a fool's game, too many investors continue fooling themselves into believing they are the exception. They somehow believe they can see into the future and predict when it will be the best time to be in or out of the market, which funds will perform the best, and which asset categories will be in and out of favor.

So, where are the markets headed? Which mutual funds and asset classes will be the best? My answer is always the same, "I don't know." What I do know is that successful investing requires patience and adherence to time-proven policies and processes. And the first step in developing a successful investment portfolio is admitting to yourself that you cannot reliably predict the future, and that no one else can either. For some investors these words go down hard. However, the fact is that some things cannot be known in advance. And one of those things is the direction of the market.

A more prudent approach to making investment decisions based on hunches and guesses is to hold a diversified portfolio composed of assets with dissimilar behaviors, so that the upward movement of one asset potentially offsets the downward movement of another. It is this dissimilarity in patterns of returns of the various asset classes over time that are likely to maximize your chances of investment success while keeping your risk under control.

Notes

Notes

Chapter 4
Stocks and Bonds

The Real Risk of Investing in Stocks

Most investors know that over the long term, stocks have historically provided higher returns than bonds. Over the past century stocks had an average return of 10.8 percent compared to only 5.6 percent for bonds. Many have seen the colorful charts and graphs demonstrating how an initial $1,000 in stocks made at the beginning of 1906 would have grown to $28.6 million by the end of 2006. The problem is that these charts and graphs, used in thousands of brokerage offices and financial planning firms, and in many books and investment seminars, are based on calendar years. And measuring investment performance from January 1 to December 31 each year does not tell the full story about bear markets and the impact they can have on your portfolio. Since 1906, there have only been five calendar years (1930, 1931, 1937, 1974, and 2002) when the market has lost 20 percent or more its value, giving the impression that bear markets occur about once every twenty years.

The problem is that these charts and graphs disguise the fact that stock market losses occur much more often, and are much more significant, than investors have been led to believe.

As the accompanying chart shows, over the last one hundred years, the U.S. stock market as measured by the Dow Jones Industrial Average has experienced twenty-three investment periods, (about once every 4.5 years), in which it lost an average of not 20 percent, but **…35 percent of its value**.

Past Bear Markets		
Starting Date	**Ending Date**	**Loss**
01/19/1906	11/15/1907	49%
11/19/1909	09/25/1911	27%
09/30/1912	07/30/1914	24%
11/21/1916	12/19/1917	40%
11/03/1919	08/24/1921	47%
09/03/1929	11/13/1929	48%
04/17/1930	07/08/1932	86%
09/07/1932	02/27/1933	37%
02/05/1934	07/26/1934	23%
03/10/1937	03/31/1938	49%
11/12/1938	04/08/1939	23%
09/12/1939	04/28/1942	40%
05/29/1946	05/17/1947	23%
12/13/1961	06/26/1962	27%
02/09/1966	10/07/1966	25%
12/03/1968	05/26/1970	36%
01/11/1973	12/06/1974	45%
09/21/1976	02/28/1978	27%
04/27/1981	08/12/1982	24%
08/25/1987	10/19/1987	36%
07/17/1990	10/11/1990	21%
01/14/2000	09/21/2001	30%
03/19/2002	10/09/2002	32%

In light of the chart above, it's surprising to me that anyone would invest 100 percent of their life savings in stocks. Letting bear markets devour your hard-earned cash does not make sense. People who are approaching their years before retirement simply don't have time to recover from 30 or 35 percent losses in their retirement savings. These high levels of loss come along all too often and can take too long to recover.

The truth is that if you invest in stocks long enough, either directly or through mutual funds, you will at some point lose money. And you have two ways to help protect your retirement savings from significant stock market declines. The first is by successfully timing the market. The second is by adding high-quality bonds to your portfolio.

Who Needs Bonds?

If you look at the last sixty-plus years of history, stocks have earned 11.4 percent versus 5.6 percent for bonds, thereby raising the question, if stocks earn about twice as much as bonds, why invest in bonds? One reason is that stocks can also be the worst financial asset as well. Anyone who invested in the stock market between April 2000 and March 2003 can attest to that. During this bear market, stocks as measured by the S&P 500 lost 44 percent of their value.

Stock market losses may seem insignificant if you have only $5,000 invested, but what about a retirement savings portfolio of $500,000. Every time the market falls 10 percent, you have lost $50,000. Now, imagine the market slowly losing 40 percent over the next several months or years, and you have now lost $200,000. The investment industry mantra that says you should "stay the course" and "think long term" while you are in the middle of losing 25 or 30 percent of your hard-earned retirement savings in stocks can be financially as well as emotionally devastating to an investor of any age.

To achieve one's financial goals, investors need to find a way to keep losses small enough so that the losses won't cause them to abandon their long-term investment strategy. Since 1946, the stock market has experienced ten major corrections, or bear markets. On average, those downturns cost investors about 27 percent of the value of their investments.

So, how can one find a way to protect his or her savings during periods of significant stock market declines? You don't do it by bailing out of stocks, but by having enough of your portfolio invested in bonds. One of the biggest mistakes investors make, however, is comparing the returns of stocks and bonds. The fact is that bonds are not stocks. Bonds are not meant to make you rich. Bonds are meant to provide investors with gains of about 5 to 6 percent a year, while keeping money relatively safe during periods of stock market declines. The following chart shows how evident this was over the last sixty years. During the ten markets in which stocks lost an average of 27 percent of their value, bonds gained an average of 11.3 percent.

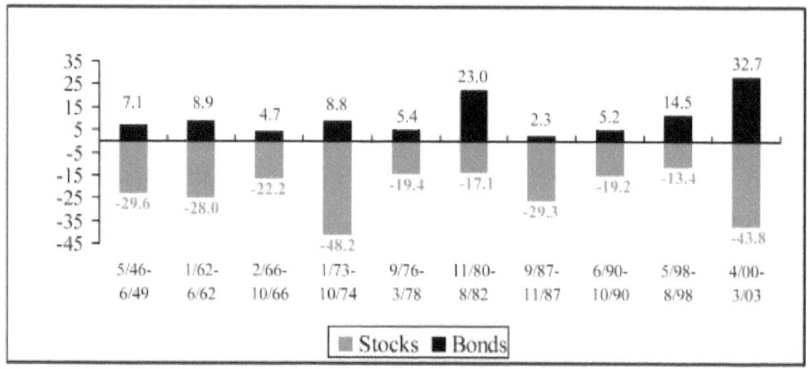

Data: Stocks; S&P 500 Index, Bonds; Intermediate-
Term Government / Corporate Bond Index

Considering the financial goals of most individuals, investing in stocks and bonds should not be an either/or decision. Unfortunately, many investors still think of bonds as an investment only for retirees looking to receive an income. However, having a core holding of various bond and stock funds can help those saving for retirement, as well as those withdrawing money during retirement to build and/or preserve capital at a more consistent and steady rate in both bull and bear markets.

Shorter Is Better

Most investors know that when interest rates rise, bond prices fall. Does this mean you should bail on bonds in the current rising-rate climate? Not at all! When you and your financial advisor plotted an investment strategy, you considered at least three critical factors—

your financial goals, time horizon, and attitudes about risk. It's not likely that your advisor said, "Oh, by the way, if interest rates rise, this strategy is toast." While rising interest rates might tempt some investors to cut back on bond allocations, there are more compelling reasons to stay the course and adopt defensive strategies to mitigate interest rate exposure to fixed income portfolios. One of the biggest reasons is that bond funds help to reduce volatility and losses. Second, bond funds provide income.

At face value, an increase in interest rates may seem like a good deal for bond investors. After all, who wouldn't like to receive more investment income? But interest rate increases mostly benefit those who are looking to invest in bonds rather than those holding bonds. Why is this? When interest rates go down, new bonds are introduced to the market with lower yields than older bonds, driving the demand—and the price—for older bonds higher. Similarly, when interest rates rise, newer bonds may offer higher yields than older bonds, driving the price for older bonds down. This inverse relationship between interest rates and bond prices is what's known as, as interest rate risk. Generally, the longer the maturity of a bond or duration of a bond fund, the greater the risk of price volatility and, consequently, interest rate risk. However, investors can significantly reduce this risk without reducing returns by investing in a bond portfolio consisting of intermediate-term bonds, rather than long-term bonds.

Many investors are under the false impression they will get short-changed by the lower yields of intermediate-term bonds. However, on a risk return adjusted basis, intermediate-term bonds have historically been a better investment than long-term bonds.

From 1926 through 2004, Long Term Government Bonds had an average annualized return of 5.5 percent, versus 5.4 percent for Intermediate Term Government Bonds. This additional return of one tenth of 1 percent, however, came at a price. Long Term Government Bonds experienced twenty-one calendar year losses, as well as a worst one-year loss of -9.2 percent, a three-year loss of -14.1 percent, a five-year loss of -10.3 percent, and a ten-year loss of -1.1 percent. Intermediate Term Government Bonds, however, experienced only eight calendar year losses, and never had a negative return in any three-, five-, or ten-year investment period (see chart).

1926-2006	Long-Term Bonds	Intermediate-Term Bonds
Average Return	5.5%	5.4%
Total # losing yrs.	21	8
Worst 1 Year	-9.2%	-5.1%
Worst 3 Years	-14.1%	+4.9%
Worst 5 Years	-10.3%	+6.5%
Worst 10 Years	-1.1%	+13.9%

Intermediate-Term Government Bonds based on Five-Year Treasury Notes Long-Term Government Bonds measured using a bond portfolio of 20 years.
Source: Ibbotson Associates

During this period, Intermediate Term Government Bonds earned 98 percent of the return of Long Term Government bonds (5.4 percent versus 5.5 percent), with 42 percent less volatility.

Notes

Notes

Chapter 5
Risk Tolerance

Much like the stock market, the game show *Deal or No Deal* taps into the most basic emotion of investors: greed. Contestants walk on stage saying how they would be happy to make enough money to buy a home or send their kids to college. Halfway through the game, they find themselves up $200,000, providing them with enough money to buy that home or send their children to college. But somewhere along the way, greed grabs a hold of them, and they find themselves shouting, "no-deal," searching for that elusive one million dollar case, which for most eventually leads to financial disaster.

Many people invest in the stock market with the same kind of attitude as the contestants of *Deal or No Deal*. Most investors know that over the long term, stocks have historically provided higher returns than bonds. Many have seen the colorful charts and graphs demonstrating how an initial $1,000 in stocks made at the beginning of 1926 would have grown to $2,710,000 by the end of 2005, while bonds were worth only $63,200. However, simply investing in stocks without regard of a possible bear market can result in financial disaster later. Regardless of your age or your years to retirement, losing money while sitting in stock funds during protracted bear markets destroys confidence and unnecessarily erodes account values.

Even if you thought you'd be willing to sit through a decline like that if and when it occurred, when it actually happens in real time, with your real money on the line in your own personal retirement account, you would more than likely not be able to summon the emotional fortitude and courage to stomach the financial damage.

Contrary to what Wall Street and the financial media would like you to believe, no one should ever feel compelled to invest outside of their risk tolerance level. There is more to life than simply plowing money into stocks and hoping for the best in ten or twenty years. You also should be able to sleep at night, play with your kids, go to work, and enjoy life without constantly worrying about your investments.

Finding Your Comfort Zone

The first conversation we have at Capital Wealth Management with any potential new client during our portfolio review session is about risk. It's the most basic part of investing, the topic that most of the industry (and most investors) would be happy to avoid altogether. Let me be blunt about this: Spending the time to understand your risk tolerance is one of the most crucial steps to successful long-term investing. Investors who don't understand risk can't understand the decisions and choices they must make. If you are not comfortable with your portfolio's level of risk and losses, you will never earn your portfolio's level of gains. Your tolerance for risk isn't a good or a bad thing; it's just who you are. It does not matter how low or high your risk tolerance level is, as long as you know what it is. And once you identify your risk tolerance level, you can then create and build an investment portfolio of stocks and bonds that you can be financially as well as emotionally comfortable with in all markets.

When it comes to investing, there is no perfect way to know in advance precisely what level of loss one may be willing to accept, but there are ways to help investors get a better handle on it. In our investment seminars and in working with clients, we often use a table of numbers to show the results in the past of various combinations of stocks (as represented by the S&P 500 Index) and bonds (five-year Treasuries), each with its own set of returns of risk. With this table, an investor who has carefully thought about his or her needs and risk tolerance can choose a combination of investments that is likely to provide the right combination of growth and comfort.

Stocks	Bonds	Worst 1 Year	Worst 5 Years	Average Return
0%	100%	-5.5%	16.3%	5.6%
10%	90%	-4.7%	20.2%	5.9%
20%	80%	-7.7%	17.4%	6.4%
30%	70%	-12.3%	13.7%	6.8%
40%	60%	-15.0%	10.0%	7.5%
50%	50%	-20.4%	6.2%	7.9%
60%	40%	-24.7%	2.3%	8.4%
70%	30%	-28.8%	-1.5%	9.0%
80%	20%	-32.5%	-5.4%	9.6%
90%	10%	-35.6%	-9.3%	10.1%
100%	0%	-38.9%	-17.5%	10.5%

Stocks represented by the S&P 500 Index, Bonds represented by five-year Treasuries.

Each line in the table details what the results would have been over the last forty years of various combinations of stocks and equities. The columns are arranged in increasing order of risk, with the least aggressive, 100 percent bonds, at the top, and the most aggressive, 100 percent stocks, at the bottom. The way to use this table is to find a column that you could be financially and emotionally comfortable with.

For example, if you are conservative, and avoiding losses is a high priority for you, find the column that has a one-year loss that you think you could live with. If 15 percent is the most you are willing to give up during any twelve-month period, and you are willing to earn a minimum cumulative return of 10 percent after five years, that suggests you might be comfortable in a portfolio of 40 percent stocks and 60 percent bonds. As you travel across to the last column, you will find that this asset allocation has produced an average return of 7.5 percent. So, the next logical question is, would a return of 7.5 percent get you where you want to go? If a return of 7.5 percent is enough to meet your objectives within your risk tolerance level, that's a good sign that you've found a portfolio that is right for you. Most investors find that there's a disparity between their desired or needed annual return, and the losses they would be willing to accept. Their first impulse is to usually go for their desired return and figure they will "hang in there" through the bad markets, which is usually a big mistake.

If your need for return and risk straddles two columns, choosing risk over return is usually the more appropriate choice for two reasons. First, the figures in this table are not predictions of the future, only results from the past. And the past is a more reliable indicator of risk than of returns. For any given combination of stocks and bonds, the pattern of volatility will be more constant and predictable than the pattern of return. Second, risk matters much more than most people think. After all, if we are not willing to accept our portfolio's potential level of volatility and losses, how can we "honestly" expect to earn our portfolio's potential level of gains?

Notes

Notes

Chapter 6
Asset Allocation—The Key to Successful Investing

If you knew that more than 90 percent of the performance of your portfolio could be attributed to just one factor, would you want to know what that factor is? If I say, "asset allocation," what does that mean to you? If you are like most investors, it doesn't mean much. Chances are you think it's simply a fancy term that investment advisors throw around to try to sound intelligent when they talk about managing money. Well, the fact is that asset allocation is the single most important critical component of investing success. I know that flies in the face of most everything you see, hear, and read about in the financial media and investment magazines. However, numerous studies and Nobel Prize-winning research over the last fifty years clearly show that more than 90 percent of the performance of your retirement or child's college savings portfolio will be determined by your asset allocation decision. In other words, asset allocation will have more to do with the success or failure of your portfolio than finding the best-performing individual investments. To some of you, that last sentence may make absolutely no sense. After all, what matters more than finding the best stocks or mutual funds? Consider the following hypothetical example.

You have $1,000 to invest in 1977, and you decide to buy Berkshire Hathaway stock. The share price is $100, and you purchase one share, placing the rest of your money ($900) into a savings account that earns 4 percent per year. Your asset allocation is 10 percent stocks, and 90 percent cash. Thirty years later, your savings account is worth $2,955, and your Berkshire Hathaway stock is worth, $109,990. Your total portfolio has a value of $112,945. Not bad! But if you had instead invested 90 percent of your money ($900) into Berkshire Hathaway stock and 10 percent ($100) into the savings account, your portfolio with an asset allocation of 90 percent stocks and 10 percent cash would be worth 2,740,835. The difference between the two portfolios was not the individual investments, but rather the asset allocation of them.

Whatever your investment goals are, achieving them starts with making investment decisions based on things you can control, rather than things over which you have no control. Asset allocation:

- Keeps your portfolio within your risk tolerance level
- Means you will have no reason to continue wasting your time watching CNBC
- Saves you from second-guessing yourself
- Means you can ignore most everything you see, hear, and read in the financial media about investing
- Works in both bull and bear markets
- Means you will no longer be making investment decisions based on predictions
- Means you will be managing your money based on a time-tested, proven-effective, investment strategy
- Reduces most of the risk of investing
- Increases the probability of achieving your financial goals

Asset Allocation in Action

One of the most important yet least understood aspects of portfolio management is asset allocation. Asset allocation is the cornerstone of a prudent investment plan and is the single most important decision that an investor will make in regard to a portfolio. Several decades of academic research has consistently demonstrated that adding several different asset classes in a portfolio can create an efficient set of investments that work together to achieve your financial goals with less risk and higher expected return.

The accompanying chart shows that from 1970 through 2007 the S&P 500 Index had an annualized return of 11.2 percent, while the diversified portfolio of stocks and bonds had an annualized return of 11.3 percent. The all-equity S&P 500 Index experienced one- and three-year losses of -26.5 and -37.6 percent, respectively. However, as a result of the bonds in the diversified portfolio, the worst one-year loss was -13.2 percent, and the worst three-year loss was only -8.5 percent. In other words, the 60/40 portfolio provided a return that equaled the performance of the U.S. stock market while reducing the risk by more than 40 percent.

Allocation	60% Stocks 40% Bonds	S&P 500
U.S. large growth stocks	7.5%	50%
U.S. large value stocks	7.5	50
U.S. small growth stocks	7.5	0
U.S. small value stocks	7.5	0
International large stocks	12.5	0
International small stocks	12.5	0
Emerging Markets	5.0	0
Bonds	40.0	0
Annual Return	**11.8%**	**11.2%**
Worst 1 Year loss	**-13.2**	**-26.5**
Worst 3 Year loss	**-8.5**	**-37.6**

100% stock portfolio represented by the S&P 500 Index; *Diversified Portfolio represented by the following indices: U.S. Small-Growth (Russell 2000 Growth), U.S. Small-Value (Russell 2000 Value), S&P 500 (U.S. Large-Growth), International large stocks (MSCI EAFE). U.S. Large-Value stocks (S&P/BARRA Value) International small stocks (MSCI EAFE NDTR_D), Emerging Markets (MSCI Select Emerging Markets index). Bonds (Lehman Brothers Aggregate Bond)

The importance of asset allocation, or deciding what percentage of a portfolio to devote to various asset classes, cannot be overstated. Unfortunately, the most important decision to achieving financial success is also the least understood. Investors spend too much of their time and money picking individual stocks and mutual funds, and too little time deciding which asset class of investments they should own.

Achieving one's financial goals starts with making investment decisions based on things you can control, rather than on things over which you have no control. And asset allocation has more control over your portfolio's chances of success than any other investment decision you will make.

The Benefits of Rebalancing

As the market moves up and down over time, the way your money is distributed among different types of investments—your asset allocation—changes. Before you know it, your mix of investments can be much different than it was when you started out. Rebalancing your portfolio can help lower your portfolio's level of volatility while stabilizing returns. For instance, imagine you decided the best way to split your retirement savings of $100,000 was 50/50 between stocks and bonds. If the stock market rises, the growing value of your stock funds could shift the allocation of your portfolio to 70 percent stocks ($70,000) and 30 percent bonds ($30,000)—which means your portfolio is now subject to more risk than you intended. And as we saw through the bear market of 2000-2002, a portfolio of 70 percent stocks and 30 percent bonds lost 19.8 percent versus 5.8 percent for a portfolio of 50 percent stocks and bonds.

To rebalance the previous portfolio to its desired 50-50 allocation of stocks and bonds, an investor would have to sell $20,000 of stocks and buy an equal amount of bonds to restore the portfolio to its original level of risk. However, unless the rebalancing occurs in a nontaxable account, taxes will be due on the capital gain realized on the sale of the $20,000 of stocks. If taxes are not an issue, as with tax-deferred accounts such as IRAs, there is no reason not to rebalance one's portfolio. To avoid a hefty tax bill in taxable accounts, you might be able to sell losing investments to offset your gains. Therefore, an investor must exercise judgment when weighing the benefits of rebalancing against the taxes generated.

Rebalancing accomplishes five important objectives:

Returns your portfolio to its original asset mix
Forces you to buy low and sell high
Locks in gains you have made
Forces you to avoid speculating
Keeps your portfolio within your risk level

Rebalancing is not the same as market timing, which involves attempting to predict future market directions in pursuit of short-term performance, and rarely works to the investor's benefit. In contrast, portfolio rebalancing forces you to trim back on winners and increase undervalued categories—a principal of buy low, sell high. However, many investors do just the opposite—they chase the best performing funds and end up buying high and selling low, which of course significantly increases the volatility (risk) of their portfolio.

A properly allocated portfolio is made up of investments that don't all move the same way at the same time. However, sometimes this will lead to a portfolio that's gotten too far away from your original allocation. By occasionally rebalancing your portfolio, you'll ensure that you stick to your original plans and have the kind of discipline that leads to long-term success.

Notes

Notes

Chapter 7
Reducing Volatility

Most investors spend their lives focused on increasing their investment returns. But focusing on maximizing your returns hides the critical role that reducing investment losses and volatility can have on your portfolio. What's unnerving about the math behind investment losses is that many investors do not realize how much risk they are taking when they choose to put their money in volatile investments. Below are three reasons why avoiding investment losses is the key to successful investing.

1. **Any percentage loss requires a larger percentage gain to recover.** When people experience a loss, they naturally think about the return necessary to earn it back. When your investments experience a certain percentage loss, you will need a larger percentage gain to get back to even. For instance, if your $100,000 portfolio loses 10 percent, it must subsequently earn about 11.1 percent to fully recover to its original pre-loss level. In dollar terms, a 10 percent loss reduces your portfolio to $90,000, but a 10 percent rebound lifts the portfolio to only $99,000. You need an 11.1 percent increase to reach $100,000.

2. **The return needed to recover from a loss grows disproportionately higher as the loss increases.** For every percent loss level, a larger

percentage gain is required to return the portfolio to its original value. This is because you have less money working for you after a loss (see chart). For instance, the 10 percent loss from the previous example required a return of 11.1 percent to recover. However; a 25 percent loss requires a return of 33.3 percent to get back even; a 50 percent loss requires a 100 percent return; and a 75 percent loss needs a 400 percent return. The following chart demonstrates that recovering from a percentage loss requires a larger subsequent percentage gain … *just to break even.*

There are two rules to investing. "Rule No. 1 is to never lose money. Rule No. 2 is to never forget rule number one." *Warren Buffet, Chairman of Berkshire Hathaway"*

Investment loss	Return Needed to Breakeven
-10%	+11%
-20%	+25%
-33%	+50%
-50%	+100%
-75%	+400%

3. It's not only the money you lose, but also the time you lose trying to get your money back. If you have $100,000 and experience a 10 percent loss, you would need an average return of 9 percent over the next fifteen months to get your portfolio back to its original $100,000 value. With a 33 percent loss, you would need an average annual return of 9 percent over the following four and a half years to get back to even. Should you lose 50 percent, it would take more than *eight years to recover from your losses.*

Reducing Volatility Can Increase Savings

When it comes to investing, most investors focus their attention on averages. The thinking goes, the higher the average return, the better. The problem is that when it comes to comparing the performance of two mutual funds or portfolios, relying on average returns (adding the annual returns and dividing by the number of years invested) can be extremely misleading. The reason, average returns do not factor in the significant impact that volatility can have on investment performance. In terms of investing, volatility measures the amount by which annual returns vary or deviate from average returns. The greater the range of those returns the greater the volatility.

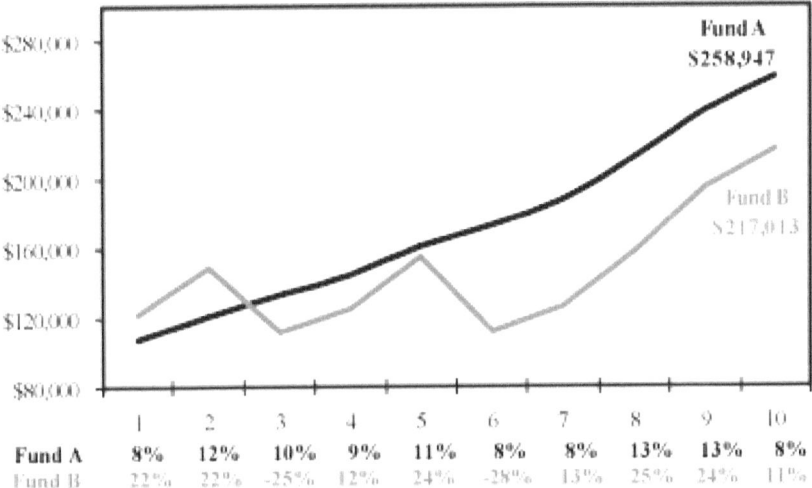

To illustrate the impact volatility can have on investment performance, let's consider you have $100,000 to invest, with a choice of two mutual funds, A and B. Each fund has the exact average return of 10 percent over the next ten years. Which would you choose? The answer provided by the vast majority of people we pose this question to at our investment workshops is, "It doesn't matter. Since they both have the same 'average' return; they could choose either portfolio and have the exact same outcome." However, that is not always the case. As the following chart shows, Fund A and Fund B performed equally well (in terms of average returns), but their performance was anything but equal.

Despite the fact that Fund B had the same average return and outperformed Fund A in eight of the ten years, Fund A ended up with $42,000 more than Fund B. If these were two actual mutual funds, which fund do you think the financial magazines would be touting?

Which fund do you think brokers would be selling? The fund with five years of 20-plus returns, or the fund with a highest one year return of only 13 percent?

Contrary to what we are led to believe, successful investing is not about trying to achieve the highest average return. Average returns reviewed without any reference to risk and volatility are useless. You need to know the risk that was taken to get those returns, because in the end the only thing that matters is your retirement portfolio's dollar returns, not its average return.

Decreasing Volatility Increases Retirement Income

The ultimate goal of any retirement income plan is to determine how much of an investment portfolio a retiree can safely withdraw each year to provide them with their desired level of income in retirement. If retirees withdraw too much from their retirement portfolio too early, they will exhaust their retirement savings prematurely. Conversely, if they withdraw too little, they will lower their standard of living needlessly.

In the previous chapter I discussed how important reducing volatility and losses is for someone saving money for retirement. However, volatility and investment losses, even over the short term, can increase a retirees chances of running out of money in retirement.

The accompanying graph shows the significant impact that volatility and losses can have on a portfolio during retirement. Portfolios A and B both start with $500,000 in retirement savings, withdraw an initial (8 percent) $40,000 of income in year one, and $40,000 each year thereafter. However, this is where the similarities end. After nineteen years, Portfolio A has run out of money, while Portfolio B is still worth $432,000 after twenty years.

	Portfolio A 10%		Portfolio B 9%	
Yr	Avg. Return	Ending Balance	Avg. Return	Ending Balance
1	6%	$490,000	5%	$485,000
2	14	518,600	12	503,200
3	-6	447,484	2	473,264
4	-19	322,462	-5	409,600
5	11	317,932	10	410,560
6	9	306,546	8	403,405
7	2	272,677	11	407,780
8	11	265,399	10	408,558
9	14	262,554	13	421,671
10	7	240,933	5	402,754
11	14	234,664	12	411,085
12	-5	182,930	5	391,639
13	-6	131,954	0	351,639
14	18	115,706	17	371,418
15	27	106,946	16	390,844
16	14	81,918	13	401,654
17	30	41,788	12	409,853
18	23	11,400	11	414,937
19	26	**Broke!**	14	433,028
20	10		9	**432,000**

What makes this outcome even more amazing is the fact that Portfolio A:

- Had a higher average return than Portfolio B
- Had the same amount of money withdrawn each year as Portfolio B
- Outperformed Portfolio B in 15 of the 20 years
- Ran out of money in year 19, while Portfolio B was still worth $432,000 at the end of year 20

In 1995, Fidelity Legend Peter Lynch, former portfolio manager of the Magellan Fund, told readers of Worth Magazine they could invest 100 percent of their money in stocks (based on their historical 10 percent average return) and safely withdraw an initial 7 percent a year, adjusting for inflation, and never run out of money. Various studies proved it wasn't safe. Relying on simple average returns as Mr. Lynch did, failed to factor in the damage that volatility and investment losses can have on a portfolio during the distribution phase of investing. Following his advice put retirees in danger of going broke. Mr. Lynch later acknowledged the error when it was brought to his attention. Unfortunately, far too many smart people today are still under the same assumption as Mr. Lynch was then, that as long as their portfolio's rate of return is higher than the rate of withdrawal, they will never have to worry about running out of money.

The primary objective for most individuals in retirement is not trying to become rich; it's avoiding ever having to worry about becoming poor. Unfortunately, far too many retirees are still under the assumption that as long as their portfolio's rate of return is higher than rate of withdrawal, they will never have to worry about running out of money. And as we have seen, reaching for higher investment returns increases volatility, which can increase a retiree's chances of running out of money. That is why it is critical for retirees and those approaching retirement to realize that managing money during retirement is completely different than managing money for retirement. The goal now is no longer achieving the highest returns, but developing a portfolio with the right mix of assets that can provide them with the "returns they need," with as "little volatility" as possible.

You could spend as much time in retirement as you have spent saving for it. And for retirees seeking a lifetime of retirement income, it is essential to not only get the right mix of assets that can provide them with the returns they need, but also with a level of volatility that's as low as possible.

Are You Leaving Your Retirement to Luck?

Most people understand that the sooner they begin saving for retirement the better. Putting money aside now, rather than later, means that you will have more assets in the long run. However saving for retirement and having a plan for your retirement savings are two different things. Blindly saving money in a 401(k), 403(b), or IRA, and hoping that it will somehow "all work out in the end," is not a plan.

Consider that this is the year you have finally decided to have your dream house built. Before construction begins, you sit down with your builder to review the blueprints. To your surprise, he tells you he doesn't work that way. Rather than plan ahead, he prefers to buy the lumber and building materials first and build the house as he goes along. Most of us would be reluctant to hire such a builder. Unfortunately, most investors follow the same approach when it comes to saving for their retirement.

According to a recent Retirement Confidence Survey conducted by the Employee Benefit Research Institute, many Americans' retirement expectations "are like a piece of Swiss cheese—full of holes." The survey demonstrated that most individuals expect to have a comfortable retirement even though most have made no estimate of how much savings they will need to live comfortably once they retire. According to the study, two-thirds of survey respondents said they are "confident" they will have enough money to live comfortably in retirement. When asked if they knew how much money they needed to live comfortably in retirement, 66 percent had no idea. The results of this survey are disturbing but not surprising. In fact, I believe it is probably closer to 96 percent rather than 66 percent of investors who have no idea how much savings they need to live comfortably in retirement.

In my ten years of working with hundreds of different individual investors, I never recall even one individual who knew the amount of savings they would need to support their desired level of lifestyle when they retire. Too many investors choose to skip right over the boring planning process and head straight for the sexy stuff: picking mutual funds. Choosing mutual funds without knowing what your goals are is like putting the cart before the horse.

The fact is that:

- If you don't know how much savings you need to live comfortably in retirement, how can you know how much you need to save for retirement?
- If you don't know how much you need to save for retirement, how can you know what rate of return you need on your investments?
- If you don't know what rate of return you need on your investments, how can you know how much risk you need to take?
- If you don't know how much risk you need to take, how can you know how much of your savings should be in stocks and bonds?
- If you don't know how much of your savings should be in stocks and bonds, how can you possibly know which mutual funds you should invest in?

Ask yourself these three questions. Do you know how much income you will need annually to retire comfortably? Do you know if you are saving enough each year to retire? Do you know what rate of return you need on your investments? If your answer to all three questions is not a resounding yes, you are leaving your lifestyle in retirement to luck. If your answer to all three questions is yes, chances are you have a written investment plan.

Having a written investment plan can significantly increase your chances of living the lifestyle you want in retirement. Having a written investment plan helps you to decide exactly what your objectives are and establishes guidelines for achieving them. Creating a written investment plan forces you and/or your advisor to put an investment strategy in writing and commit to a disciplined investment plan. At Capital Wealth Management, we create a written investment plan for every client. A written investment plan should be a detailed plan, not a general statement. The key components of an investment plan should include such things as:

- Your investment goals and time horizons
- The minimum amount of savings needed to achieve goals
- How much income you can safely withdraw in retirement
- The average annual return needed to accomplish those goals
- The types of investments you will and won't include
- How the assets are to be allocated within your portfolio
- The rebalancing procedures of your investments
- The risk level of the portfolio

The bottom line is that without an investment plan, no matter how your investments are performing, you never know whether you are on track to achieve your financial goals. When you, and/or your financial advisor take the time to develop an investment plan, you have less worry and more peace of mind, knowing that you have a strategy in place designed to increase the probability of providing you with the savings you need to live comfortably in your retirement years.

How Big Does that Nest Egg Need to Be?

Most people look forward to spending their retirement years doing things they didn't have the time, money, or both of during their working years. Now that they have the time, that leaves on big question, how big should their nest egg be? A lot of financial advice touts the figure of 70 or 80 percent of final working income before retirement as to what one will need for income in retirement. The flaw with this calculation is that everyone's idea of the perfect retirement is different. To some, retirement could be playing golf every day. To others, it could be tending to their garden. Some people may want to travel and dine out more. As a result, the amount of income one will need in retirement could be significantly higher or lower than 70 or 80 percent of one's final working income.

A better way to determine how much in retirement savings you will need in the future is by deciding how much retirement income you would need if you were to retire today. In other words, if you plan on having no mortgage, college tuition payments, or credit card debt in the future, do not include any mortgage, college tuition payments, or credit card debt you may currently have in your calculations.

Let's assume that you determined you would need $80,000 of income to support your desired level of lifestyle if you retired today. Chances are that you won't have to rely on your portfolio for the whole $80,000. You'll probably have Social Security, or you may have a pension or other sources of income you can rely on such as rental income from real estate. In our example, all those sources of income add up to $30,000 a year. That leaves you with a "shortfall" of $50,000 of income that must come from your retirement savings. At this point you can start to get a good handle on your retirement picture. A quick rule of thumb is to now multiply the annual income needed from your retirement savings by 20, which in this case means you would need a minimum of $1 million in savings. (See accompanying chart)

| | Desired Level of Annual Income (in today's dollars) | | | |
	$25,000	$50,000	$75,000	$100,000
	Retirement Savings Needed			
In 1 Year	$500,000	$1.0 million	$1.5 million	$2.0 million
In 5 Years	$595,000	$1.2 million	$1.8 million	$2.4 million
In 10 Years	$705,000	$1.4 million	$2.1 million	$2.8 million
In 15 Years	$839,000	$1.7 million	$2.5 million	$3.4 million

What if you wanted to retire in say ten or fifteen years from now? Assuming an average inflation rate of 3.5 percent, it will take $70,530 of annual income in ten years and $83,767 in fifteen years to purchase the same amount of goods that $50,000 can purchase today. You would need to have $1.4 million in savings in ten years and $1.7

million in savings in fifteen years to provide an annual income equal to $50,000 in *today's dollars.*

If the chart above indicates a significant gap between the annual income you will need and the amount of savings you are likely to have in retirement, you may need to consider changing your rate of savings, your current investment portfolio, your lifestyle in retirement, or some combination of all three.

Saving for College

Next to buying a home and saving for retirement, a college education is the largest expenditure most parents will ever make. According to The College Board's Trends in College Pricing 2006, the average annual cost of tuition, fees, room, and board at a four-year public institution was $12,796 for the academic year 2006–2007. For a private institution, the cost was $30,367. Public colleges and universities experienced a 5.6 percent tuition increase from the prior year, 2005–2006, while private colleges and universities experienced a 5.7 percent tuition increase.

Just how much will your child's college education cost? The chart below shows the approximate annual cost of tuition, as well as room and board, for a four-year undergraduate education based on the year a child will enter a public or private institution. For example, a six-year-old in 2008 will face college costs that will be nearly double what they are today upon entering college twelve years later in 2020.

Child's age In 2008	Yrs Until College	School Year	Public College	Private College
18	-	2008	$14,269	$33,863
17	1	2009	$15,068	$35,759
16	2	2010	$15,912	$37,762
15	3	2011	$16,803	$39,877
14	4	2012	$17,744	$42,110
13	5	2013	$18,738	$44,468
12	6	2014	$19,787	$46,958
11	7	2015	$20,895	$49,588
10	8	2016	$22,065	$52,364
9	9	2017	$23,301	$55,297
8	10	2018	$24,606	$58,394
7	11	2019	$25,983	$61,664
6	12	2020	$27,439	$65,117
5	13	2021	$28,975	$68,763
4	14	2022	$30,598	$72,614
3	15	2023	$32,311	$76,680
2	16	2024	$34,121	$80,974
1	17	2025	$36,031	$85,509

Now that you have a good idea how much it may cost to send your child to college, how will you accumulate the savings you need to afford it? Unfortunately, many parents we initially meet with appear more concerned about investing in a college saving plan that can potentially minimize their taxes, (i.e., 529 plans, Coverdell accounts, and UGMA accounts, etc.) rather than having an investment strategy in place that can maximize the probability of accumulating the savings they will need to pay for their child's college education. If there is one thing we have had drummed into our heads, it is that saving on taxes is the name of the game. Yes, investment strategies should take into account tax breaks available to investors. However, as important as minimizing taxes may be, it should never be the primary factor in one's investment decisions.

The bottom line is that when it comes to saving for your child's college education, the only thing that should matter is having an investment plan in place that can increase the probability of making sure that the amount of college savings your child needs will be there when they need it. And that has nothing to do with the college savings plan you choose. Whether you save in a 529 plan, Coverdell, or UGMA account is basically irrelevant. What will ultimately determine how successful or unsuccessful you will be in achieving your desired or anticipated level of savings will be the investment portfolio you have, not how much you save in taxes.

Who cares about tax-free withdrawals on earnings if there are not enough earnings! All of the tax savings you had along the way won't matter much when it comes time to write out the check for your child's tuition, and you can't afford to pay the bill.

Notes

Notes

Chapter 8
Mutual Fund Fees and Expenses

Over the past twenty years, American investors increasingly have turned to mutual funds to save for retirement and other financial goals. Today, with so many with 401(k) retirement plans, more than eighty million people own mutual funds. Although the goal of mutual fund companies is to make money for their investors, their ultimate goal, like any business, is to make money for themselves. For this reason, all mutual funds have annual fees and expenses. It is these fees and expenses that combine to make up a fund's expense ratio. The expense ratio tells you what percentage of your savings is being siphoned out of your account to pay for the fund's expenses each year.

	Portfolio A Annual Expenses 1.75%				Portfolio B Annual Expenses 0.25%		
Yr	Return Before Expenses	Return After Expenses	Growth of $100,000	Yr	Return Before Expenses	Return After Expenses	Growth of $100,000
1	10%	8.25%	$108,250	1	10%	9.75%	$109,750
2	10%	8.25%	$117,180	2	10%	9.75%	$120,450
3	10%	8.25%	$126,848	3	10%	9.75%	$132,194
4	10%	8.25%	$137,312	4	10%	9.75%	$145,083
5	10%	8.25%	$148,641	5	10%	9.75%	$159,229
6	10%	8.25%	$160,904	6	10%	9.75%	$174,753
7	10%	8.25%	$174,178	7	10%	9.75%	$191,792
8	10%	8.25%	$188,548	8	10%	9.75%	$210,492
9	10%	8.25%	$204,103	9	10%	9.75%	$231,015
10	10%	8.25%	$220,942	10	10%	9.75%	$253,539
11	10%	8.25%	$239,170	11	10%	9.75%	$278,259
12	10%	8.25%	$258,901	12	10%	9.75%	$305,389
13	10%	8.25%	$280,261	13	10%	9.75%	$335,165
14	10%	8.25%	$303,382	14	10%	9.75%	$367,843
15	10%	8.25%	$328,411	15	10%	9.75%	$403,708
16	10%	8.25%	$355,505	16	10%	9.75%	$443,069
17	10%	8.25%	$384,834	17	10%	9.75%	$486,269
18	10%	8.25%	$416,583	18	10%	9.75%	$533,680
19	10%	8.25%	$450,951	19	10%	9.75%	$585,714
20	10%	8.25%	**$488,155**	20	10%	9.75%	**$642,822**

For example, if you have $100,000 in a fund that maintains a 2 percent expense ratio, your expenses for the year would be $2,000, reducing your annual return by 2 percent. And since expenses are automatically subtracted from a fund's assets, you never really see what you're missing. This makes it easy to ignore the impact that mutual fees have on your return, and they can be significant over time.

The following table demonstrates how much effect mutual fund expenses can have over the long term. Portfolio A and Portfolio B both have 10 percent annual returns before expenses. Portfolio A has an expense ratio of 1.75 percent, thereby reducing its annual return to 8.25 percent. Portfolio B has annual expenses of only .25 percent, reducing its annual return to 9.75 percent. After twenty years, an original $100,000 investment in Portfolio A was worth $488,155, having lost $184,595 in expenses. However, the same $100,000 investment in Portfolio B twenty years later was worth $642,822, having lost only $29,928 in expenses. The additional $154,667 of savings (thirty percent) in Fund B was *entirely* the result of the lower expenses.

No one who owns a home would ever knowingly pay an additional 1 or 1.5 percent more for a mortgage. But that is exactly what many individuals are unknowingly doing when it comes to investing in mutual funds. Unfortunately, most investors do not know how much they are paying in expenses and how significantly expenses can impact their investment dollars.

Avoiding the December Mutual Fund "Tax Trap"

If you're thinking of buying a new mutual fund near the end of the year, you may want to hold off. Adding a mutual fund to your portfolio during the holiday season can turn out to be more expensive than anything else on your shopping list.

That's because each year, the tax law requires that mutual funds pay out taxable gains in order to qualify as a regulated investment company (RIC) under the Internal Revenue Code. Qualifying as an RIC makes the fund eligible to pass through any income and gains to shareholders without having to pay taxes at the fund level. To qualify, federal law requires mutual funds to distribute 98 percent of its ordinary and capital gain income to shareholders before the year is over. Most funds make these distributions on the ex-dividend date, which is usually in December.

On the ex-dividend date, all registered owners of the mutual fund pay taxes on any declared dividends and capital gains distributions. For the individuals who owned the fund most of the year, they at least received the Net Asset Value (NAV) appreciation that resulted from the growth of the investment, the dividends, and the realized capital gains. However, if you invest in a mutual fund just before the ex-dividend date, you can get stuck paying taxes on gains you never received. (Distributions are not taxable to tax-deferred accounts such as 401(k)s and IRAs, so purchases can be made in those accounts prior to a distribution without adverse tax consequences).

For example, let's assume you have $50,000 and buy 5,000 shares of fund XYZ with a net asset value (NAV) of $10 per share. The next day is the ex-dividend date, and the fund pays out a capital-gains distribution of $2. Although the NAV of the fund will now be reduced to $8, you still own the equivalent of $10 per share with your reinvested $2. You will now have to pay taxes on those capital gains. If half those gains are long term, taxed at 15 percent, and half are short term, taxed at 28 percent, you will pay $2,150 in taxes, even though you never received any of the appreciation of those gains, leaving you with $47,850. Adding insult to injury, if the XYZ fund is a load fund with an upfront sales charge of 5 percent ($2,500), your original $50,000 investment would now be worth only $45,460, leaving you with an immediate loss of 9 percent.

What's the alternative? To avoid this tax trap, you should first call the mutual fund company or go to their Web site to find out the fund's ex-dividend date. Waiting just a few days after the ex-dividend date to invest in the fund can now provide you with an opportunity to get in at a lower price, purchase more shares, and avoid paying any immediate tax bills.

Load Funds Make Brokers Richer and Investors Poorer

When it comes to investing in mutual funds, there are basically two flavors: load funds and no-load funds. When you invest $10,000 in a no-load fund, there is no sales commission and the entire $10,000 invested goes to work for you. In a load fund, a sales commission is subtracted from your investment. Invest $10,000 in a fund with a 5.75 percent front-end load (this is the usual arrangement for Class A shares), and only $9,425 is invested for you. That's what your account will be worth at the end of the first day you own the fund.

Another common type of load fund is Class B shares. Unlike Class A shares, which are fairly straightforward, Class B shares are a bit more complicated, and in many cases can be a bit more deceiving than Class A shares. Many commissioned advisors and brokers will tell you that there is no front-end sales charge, and that all your money goes to work for you right away, which is true. However, what many advisors and brokers fail to mention is that they also receive a commission from the fund company for selling you the fund. To pay for this upfront commission, the fund company now charges the shareholders a back-end sales load should they decide to exit the fund within a certain time period.

A typical example is a 5 percent back-end sales load that decreases by 1 percent each year until the sixth year. If you don't sell the mutual fund by then, you don't have to pay the back-end load at all. Sounds like a win-win for the broker and the investor, right? Wrong. In addition to decreasing the sales load by 1 percent each year, the fund company also passes on an additional annual expense of 1 percent to each shareholder during this period as well. Now if the shareholder doesn't sell and pay the back-end sales load, the additional annual expense of 1 percent over this six-year period will cover the sales rep commission paid out in year one. Because of these higher fees, investors can actually end up earning less money over the long term than if they paid the front-end load on an A share fund.

While not all funds have sales loads, all mutual funds do have ongoing management expenses. These include all the normal costs to run a fund and support existing shareholders: accounts, custodians, lawyers, transfer agents, printing statements, taxes, and so forth. On the whole, expense ratios range from as low as 0.2 percent for no-load index funds to as high as 2.25 percent for Class B share funds.

In the following example, let's assume you put $50,000 into each of these three funds:

1. Class A fund with a front-end load of 5.75 percent and expense ratio of 1 percent
2. Class B fund with an expense ratio of 2.25 percent
3. No-load fund with an expense ratio of .50 percent

Each fund has an average return of 10 percent before expenses and commissions. After twenty-five years, an investor in the no-load fund would have an account worth $483,418 while an investor in the Class A and Class B share funds ended up with only $406,363 and $390,540, respectively (see chart). The difference in the ending dollar value is *entirely* the result of the sales commissions and higher expenses of the load funds.

	No-Load Fund	Class A Fund	Class B *Fund
Day 1	$50,000	$47,125	$50,000
1 Yr	$54,750	$51,366	$54,000
5 yrs	$78,712	$72,508	$73,466
15 yrs	$195,066	$171,652	$168,800
25 yrs	$483,418	$406,363	$390,540

* Fund expense ratio reduced to 1.25% after year six.

The fact is that besides load funds charging a sales fee and no-load funds not, there is absolutely no difference between the two. Load funds don't attract better money managers than do no-load funds. Load funds don't have lower annual expense ratios than no-load funds. When you buy shares of a load fund, you don't get free frequent flier miles. So why would any person ever want to invest in a load fund? If there were two electronics stores side by side, and both sold the exact same television, only one charged 5 percent more to compensate the sales people, at which store would you buy your TV? With such a wide variety of no-load mutual funds available today, most investors should never pay a sales load.

If paying high expenses and commissions normally brought a higher return that investors could count on, then paying those higher expenses commissions would make sense. However, every study that

I am familiar with on mutual fund performance shows exactly the same thing: paying above-average expenses makes above-average performance less likely rather than more likely. The reason is simple. Expenses do not enhance performance, they reduce it. Every $1 you unnecessarily pay or lose now costs you not only that $1, but also the amount that $1 could earn over your investment lifetime.

Index Funds Are Anything But Average

For those who have been reading this column over the past five years, you are well aware of the fact that I am a big proponent of index funds. Yes, I am talking about boring, inexpensive, and unexciting index mutual funds. I know what you're thinking, why index funds? Index funds only provide average returns. Why should I settle for average returns in and index fund when I can achieve above average returns when I can invest in a professionally managed mutual fund?

Let's first compare the main difference between the two funds. Most mutual funds are professionally or "actively managed," An actively managed fund tries to beat the market by selecting stocks the manager hopes will outperform the index. Mutual fund shareholders pay the fund manager an annual fee of approximately 1.5% on the amount of assets they have invested in the fund in the hopes that the manager's stock and bond selections will outperform the market or index. Index funds attempt to replicate as close as possible the return of a particular benchmark, such as the S&P 500, or the Lehman Brothers Aggregate Bond Index. Unlike actively managed funds, index funds make no attempt to guess which stocks will be hot and which will be not. Index funds simply invest in all the stocks or bonds within a particular index or market. As a result, most index funds have expense ratios under 0.5 percent, and many are 0.2 percent or lower.

Actively managed funds would be worth the higher fees and expenses if they delivered superior performance compared to index funds however, numerous studies over the years have demonstrated that the vast majority of actively managed funds actually under perform index funds. One such study in the Journal of Financial Planning "The Difficulty of Selecting Superior Mutual Fund Performance", demonstrated that due to their higher costs, that on average, 80 percent of actively managed mutual funds under perform index funds each year. Increase the holding period to 20 years, and index funds outperform 89 percent of actively managed funds.

Which Mutual Funds Would You Rather Have?

	Index Mutual Funds	Actively Managed Mutual Funds
Have lower fees	√	
Have lower trading costs	√	
Are more tax-efficient	√	
Have fewer realized capital gains	√	
Never attempt to time the market	√	
Outperform on average, 80% of actively mutual funds each year	√	
Guaranteed to never under perform the market or asset class	√	
Have a 20% chance of outperforming Index Funds		√

It is truly amazing how so many people get hung up about "beating the market". Contrary to what Wall Street and CNBC would like you to believe, investing is not about outperforming the market. You are investing to earn enough money to reach your financial goals. Despite the advantages of investing in index funds, Americans put more money in actively managed mutual funds than they do in index funds. Part of the reason is because most investors think they are gifted with an above average ability to know which mutual funds will outperform the market in the future. Ask a room full of people if they consider themselves to be above average drivers and more than 80% of hands will go up. Having confidence in ones ability is a great quality to have for most things we do in our life. However, when it comes to investing, overconfidence all but guarantees, under performance.

Notes

Notes

Chapter 9
401(k)'s and IRAs

Once you leave a job, for whatever reason, you need to make a decision as to what to do with your retirement plan. If you are unsure how to deal with your 401(k) plan during the transition, you are not alone. While the Employee Benefit Research Institute (EBRI) of Washington, D.C., estimates that twenty-seven million Americans manage a combined $1 trillion in 401(k) assets, many are not clear on ground rules if they switch jobs. In fact, nearly one quarter of those responding to a recent study by Neuwirth Research Inc. were unaware of the tax consequences and penalties associated with taking a cash distribution from an employer-sponsored plan.

With all the emotions many experience after losing a job, individuals will often leave their retirement with the former employer under the impression that, one, the money is safe and, two, moving it entails one more decision at a stressful time. There is a better choice for most individuals and their families—transferring those savings into a rollover IRA. An IRA rollover is a method approved by the Internal Revenue Service (IRS) that allows you to move assets from your employer's plan into an Individual Retirement Account (IRA) without penalty—a benefit that keeps more of your retirement assets working for you and your family. The advantages of a rollover IRA include:

More Investment Choices

Rather than being limited to the number of funds or fund families within an employer's plan, an IRA provides the universe of investment choices, and owners can develop the precise mix of investments that best reflects their personal risk tolerance, investment philosophy, and financial goals.

Estate Planning Benefits

A big benefit to rolling over your 401(k) plan into an IRA is the estate planning that can be accomplished by taking advantage of what is commonly known as a "stretch-out" IRA. The IRS allows a younger beneficiary (a child, for example) to stretch distributions of an inherited IRA over his or her longer life expectancy, resulting in possibly decades of further tax deferred growth on the account. If your child is the beneficiary of your 401(k), when you die, the company will usually pay out the entire IRA to your child, triggering a taxable distribution and ending any further tax deferral.

Roth Conversion Ability

Another advantage to rolling over to your IRA is that you may then be able to convert your IRA to a Roth IRA. Your Roth IRA beneficiaries will receive the same stretch-out IRA advantages, but with the Roth IRA, your beneficiaries will be able to withdraw tax-free income for life.

Greater Control

Your previous employer may get bought out or merge with another company. The rules governing your retirement plan are largely decided by your employer. These rules may very well change when a company is merged or sold. By rolling your savings over now, you won't have to worry about losing control of your savings later.

Account Consolidation

Over the course of your career, you may change jobs several times. Companies can change locations. Some people can lose track of their paperwork and forget that their retirement savings are with one of their previous employers. When you roll over your funds after you leave your employer, especially when you consolidate your funds into one rollover account, you reduce the risk of misplacing or losing track of your money.

Whether due to retirement, career change, company layoffs or firings, leaving a job is a stressful time in anyone's life. There is a lot to consider, and worrying about what to do with your 401(k) assets just adds to this stress. If you have money in a corporate or individual qualified plan, you should make sure you are familiar with the rules governing the distribution of those assets. In most cases, an IRA rollover account will afford you and your heirs much greater flexibility.

If you have built up a large retirement account and still have the assets in a corporate plan, make sure you contact your benefits administrator to find out the rules governing distribution of retirement plan assets on behalf of your beneficiaries.

Stretching Your IRA

Whether you're age 25 or 65, planning for a financially secure future is an ongoing process. As you get closer to retirement, will you have a good understanding of how far your retirement assets will go? Will those assets take care of you and your spouse? Will there be enough left to provide a legacy to your children and their children? With proper planning, your retirement assets can help you create a source of income for not only yourself, but for your children and grandchildren as well. To create this type of legacy, you will need to apply what's known as the "stretch IRA" technique. A stretch IRA is not a special type of IRA account. A stretch IRA reflects an approach to estate planning that attempts to maximize the tax-deferred growth potential (or tax-free it it's a Roth IRA) of IRA assets by leaving them in the IRA for as long as the law permits.

The reason why I keep referring to a stretch IRA rather than a stretch 401(k), or stretch 403(b) is because the "stretch" option usually is not permitted in employer retirement plans. Even though the tax rules allow the stretch option for beneficiaries of 401(k) and 403(b) plans, most companies don't permit it. The reason is simple—the stretch can take place over decades. If the company allowed that, then they would be responsible for all the administration. There isn't any benefit to the company to do so, while it exposes them to potential liability. Instead, most company plans will cash out the beneficiaries at the death of the employee. The good news is that a surviving spouse can always roll over an employer's retirement plan into his or her own IRA. The bad news is that beneficiaries such as your children and grandchildren cannot. However, upon leaving an employer, transferring your 401(k) assets into an IRA provides the ability for these beneficiaries to receive payments from an inherited IRA during their lifetimes.

For example, a forty-year-old daughter inherits her deceased father's $500,000 of 401(k) savings paid out in the form of a lump-sum distribution from his previous employer. Since she is currently in the 30 percent tax bracket, after paying $150,000 in taxes to Uncle Sam, she is left with $350,000, which is no longer growing tax deferred. Consider the alternative. The same daughter inherits $500,000 from her deceased father's rollover IRA account. Based on her life expectancy of forty-three years, she can now stretch out her inheritance by withdrawing her required minimum distribution of one forty-third of the account value this year, then one forty-second next year, etc. Over time, the annual minimum distributions would average about 3 percent of her portfolio's value. And if her portfolio earned an average return of 8 percent, she would have a 5 percent gain of untaxed growth compounding each year. By age 68 she would have withdrawn over $850,000 of income, while still having $900,000 of tax-deferred savings left in her IRA account.

The Six Steps to Establishing a Stretch IRA:

1. Roll over your 401(k) savings into an IRA.
2. Name your spouse or someone younger as beneficiary.
3. After your death, your spouse rolls remaining assets to his or her own IRA.
4. Your spouse names a son or daughter, or both, as beneficiary
5. After your spouse's death, your son or daughter maintains the IRA and names his or her child as beneficiary.
6. Distributions continue until the beneficiary IRA is exhausted.

Some plans now offer employees the ability to take a distribution from their retirement plan upon reaching a minimum age or meeting a length of service requirement *"while they still are employed."* If you qualify for this distribution, you can elect to roll over all or a portion of these retirement assets while continuing to participate in your employer's plan without penalty. Most often, only profit-sharing 403(b) and 401(k) plans allow theses distributions.

To find out if your employer offers this in service distribution, ask your human resources or benefits department for a copy of the employer's Summary Plan Description. The Summary Plan Description explains the provisions, policies, and rules that govern your financial options.

Roth IRAs

If you are deciding to save money for retirement in an IRA account, you have a decision to make. Should you save in a Roth IRA, a deductible IRA, or a nondeductible IRA? Choosing between a deductible traditional IRA and a Roth IRA presents an interesting dilemma: tax advantage now or tax advantage later? The nondeductible traditional IRA is not nearly as difficult a decision. With a deductible IRA, contributions reduce your taxable income in the year the contribution is made, which cuts your income tax bill. But when the money is withdrawn in retirement, it counts as ordinary income and will be taxed at the same rate as income earned from a job (i.e., not at the lower long-term capital gains rate). With a Roth IRA, contributions do not reduce taxable income, so there's no deduction. However, the Roth is a tax-free account; no taxes are paid on the interest, dividends, or gains in retirement. A Roth IRA will always be a better choice than a nondeductible IRA (an IRA that is funded with after-tax dollars). Contributions in both accounts grow on a non-taxed basis, but the earnings distributed from a nondeductible IRA are taxable at regular income rates, compared to the tax-free distributions of a Roth IRA. So, the question is, do you want to cut your tax bill now or in retirement?

Let's say a married couple in the 25 percent tax bracket now and during retirement invests $4,000 each (total of $8,000) into IRAs for the next twenty-five years, and their accounts earn 8 percent a year. As the accompanying chart shows, if they saved in a Roth IRA they would have a total of $630,635 of tax-free retirement savings in twenty-five years. If they put their eight grand in deductible IRAs, they would have $630,635, but they would owe $158,000 in taxes when they withdraw the money, reducing their savings to $472,635. But wouldn't they also get a tax deduction each year? Yes, they would; in this case it would be $2,000. If they invest that $2,000 each year at 8 percent, after twenty-five years it will total $158,000. Add in that amount to their after-tax balance, and they would have $630,635 in savings, the same as the Roth IRA. So they are both the same, right? Well, not exactly.

	Deductible IRA	Roth IRA
Retirement Savings in 25 years	$630,635	$630,635
Federal Taxes	-$158,000	$0
Tax Reductions Reinvested	+$158,000	$0
Retirement Savings after taxes	$630,635	$630,635

The flaw with this analysis is that it assumes that any tax savings realized from contributing to a deductible IRA will be reinvested each year into another savings account until retirement to offset what they will pay in federal taxes. However, in the real world, anyone saving in a deductible IRA is not doing so because they plan on reinvesting their windfall from Uncle Sam each year back into another savings account for retirement. They are going to spend it. And as the second chart shows, under those circumstances, the deductible IRA in the previous example would be worth only $472,635, compared to $630,635 of tax-free retirement savings in the Roth IRA.

	Deductible IRA	Roth IRA
Retirement Savings in 25 years	$630,635	$630,635
Federal Taxes	-$158,000	$0
Tax Deductions Reinvested	+$0	$0
Retirement Savings after taxes	$472,635	$630,635

The conventional financial planning strategy of "why pay a tax today when you can pay it tomorrow" only provides a tax advantage if your tax rate in retirement is lower than your current tax rate. What if conventional wisdom is wrong, and you are not in a lower tax bracket during your retirement years? Instead of working the tax system to your advantage by deferring taxes at a high rate and paying them at a lower one, you could end up doing just the opposite.

The bottom line is that you're contributing to a retirement account to make your golden years more affordable, not to give yourself a tax break today. If you are one of the more than 90 percent of Americans eligible to have a Roth IRA, everything you save (contributions and earnings) can be withdrawn completely tax free in retirement. No matter how much you have, every penny is yours. Whether you have $500,000 or $5 million, you will never owe any taxes on any of it. If you don't want to ever take any money out, you don't have to. Uncle Sam can't even make you take any money out after age seventy and a half. And when you pass away and your money goes to your spouse or children—or to any beneficiary, for that matter—they won't have to pay taxes on any of it either.

These two IRAs do share some common characteristics. First, you can fund either the deductible or Roth with several different investment vehicles, including individual stocks, bonds, mutual funds, and CDs. Second, for tax year 2008, the contribution limit for both the deductible and Roth IRA is $5,000. Investors over fifty can contribute an extra $1,000 per year. This is basically where the similarity ends between the two IRAs. Below are seven reasons why a Roth IRA can provide most individuals saving for retirement with more benefits and flexibility than a deductible IRA.

Comparing IRAs	Deductible	Roth
Withdraw contributions tax-free	No	Yes
Age limit for contributing	Yes	No
Required distributions at 70½	Yes	No
Earnings tax-free	No	Yes
Can affect social security benefits	Yes	No
Tax-free withdrawals at 59½	No	Yes
Heirs pay taxes	Yes	No

1. Taxes

The major difference between a Roth and deductible IRA is when you get the tax break. With a deductible IRA, money does not get taxed going *in* to the account, but it is all taxed when it comes *out*. With the Roth IRA, all of the money gets taxed going *in* to the account, but none of it is taxed coming *out*. Contributions to a deductible IRA reduce your taxable income in the year the contribution is made, which cuts your income tax bill. But when the money is withdrawn in retirement, it counts as ordinary income and will be taxed at the same rate as income earned from a job (i.e., not at the lower long-term capital gains rate). With a Roth, contributions do not reduce taxable income, so there's no deduction. However, the Roth is a tax-free account; no taxes are paid on the interest, dividends, or gains—ever.

2. Required Minimum Distributions

With a deductible IRA, once you reach age seventy and a half, you must begin making annual withdrawals in certain minimum amounts. But a Roth IRA has no mandatory withdrawals. That means you can take out as little as you want as late as you want, providing for more tax-free growth while alive.

3. Beneficiaries

A Roth IRA is good for the beneficiaries of your estate. Just as you would receive the proceeds of a Roth tax-free, so would your heirs. However, beneficiaries have to pay income taxes on the money inherited from deductible IRAs.

4. Social Security

The more taxable income you receive in retirement from a deductible IRA, the more likely your Social Security benefits will also be taxed. Income from a Roth IRA, however, does not affect the calculation of whether you'll pay taxes on a portion of your retirement benefit check.

5. Liquidity

What if you want or need money before you're fifty-nine and a half? Withdrawals from a deductible IRA before the age of fifty-nine and a half can lead to taxes and penalties (except under special circumstances). This is not necessarily true for a Roth. Unlike many retirement plans, with the Roth IRA the withdrawal of contributions comes first, and contributions are always returned tax- and penalty-free, regardless of what the withdrawal is used for.

6. Home Purchase

If you're saving for a home purchase that is at least five years away and qualify as a first-time homebuyer, you can withdraw your Roth IRA contributions (tax and penalty free) in addition to $10,000 in earnings. However, with a deductible IRA, you can only withdraw a total of $10,000.

7. Contributions

Unlike a deductible IRA, contributions are permitted in a Roth IRA without regard to age. Thus, children with summer jobs can fund a Roth IRA based on their earnings. And individuals over seventy and a half who are still working can continue to fund a Roth IRA.

So here's what you're faced with in the future: you have the choice of having a regular IRA and paying a lot of taxes in the future or having a Roth IRA and paying *no taxes*. Hmmm … which IRA should you have?

Notes

Notes

Chapter 10
Choosing a Financial Advisor

In the financial world, there are basically two types of advice available to investors, brokerage accounts and advisory accounts. Unfortunately, most investors don't know the difference between these two kinds of advice. In fact, most aren't even aware a difference exists. The truth is, there's a considerable difference in financial advice and the people who dispense it. Much of the confusion surrounding the financial service differences between the two has been the result of a rule proposed in 1999 by the Securities and Exchange Commission.

The rule, called the Investment Advisers Act, has essentially allowed broker-dealers to avoid the fiduciary standards of the Investment Advisers Act of 1940. According to the act, anyone who offers fee-based management services is required to register as an investment advisor. Under previous regulations, brokers did not have to register under the Investment Company Act of 1940 so long as they did not receive any special compensation for their advice or if the advice was, in the words of the SEC, "solely incidental" to their services. However, in the late 1990s, when several large broker-dealers started offering fee-based brokerage programs, the SEC effectively removed the "solely incidental" standard by allowing brokers to hold themselves out to the public as advisers and offer extensive advisory services without being subject to the fiduciary duty and disclosure requirements of the Advisers Act. To eliminate some of this confusion and conflict of interest, the Securities and Exchange Commission now requires that all brokerage firms, or brokers who want to provide fee-based services while holding themselves out to the investing public as financial advisors, will be required to register as an investment advisor. Brokers that do not register as an investment advisor will now need to provide the following language within every new account form:

> "Your account is a brokerage account and not an advisory account. Our interests may not always be the same as yours. Please ask us questions to make sure you understand your rights and our obligations to you, including the extent of our obligations to disclose conflicts of interest and to act in your best interest. We are paid both by you and, sometimes, by people who compensate us, based on what you buy. Therefore, our profits, and our salespersons' compensation, may vary by product and over time."

Even with this disclosure, the bottom line is that advisors and brokers now offer similar services while operating under two different sets of laws. Brokers are responsible for getting the best execution of customer orders and for ensuring any trades they recommend are suitable for the customer. Advisers are subject to stricter standards that require they act in the customer's best interest. I personally believe that most investors need investment advisors.

Most of us don't perform surgery on ourselves, prosecute our own legal cases, or do root canals on our own teeth. We are perfectly happy to leave that to professionals. Yet, many people feel perfectly competent to direct their entire financial future by themselves. Unfortunately, for those of us who eventually recognize the need to work with a financial adviser, far too many wind up with brokers. I am not saying that brokers are bad people or are engaging in illegal activity. What I am saying is that brokers are salespeople, not Registered Investment Advisors. Brokers are compensated for selling products, not for solving clients' problems. The fact is that brokers ultimately keep or lose their jobs by their own performance in meeting sales targets and bringing in revenue. If their clients do well, or if their clients do poorly, is essentially irrelevant from a business perspective.

Unfortunately, most investors don't know the difference between these two kinds of advice. According to a national survey of more than one thousand investors earlier this year by the Consumer Federation of America, less than three hundred (30 percent) understood that the "primary service" provided by brokers is the buying and selling of stocks, mutual funds, bonds, etc., not investment advice. So, what is the difference between Registered Investment Advisors and brokers?

Registered Investment Advisors

Individuals and businesses that provide investment advice for a fee are required to register with the SEC and/or the states in which they do business. Registered Investment Advisors are regulated by the Investment Advisors Act of 1940. One of the key components of the Investment Advisors Act of 1940 is that Registered Investment Advisors (RIAs) have a legal, fiduciary responsibility to act in their client's best interest at all times and in all aspects of their business relationships. RIAs are also legally required to disclose all potential conflicts of interest.

Brokers

Unlike Registered Investment Advisors, brokers are not subject to a legal requirement to act as a fiduciary and are not required to disclose conflicts of interest. Brokers are salespeople, not Registered Investment Advisors. They are compensated for selling products, not for solving clients' problems. Their first loyalty is to their employer, whether it's Merrill Lynch, Morgan Stanley, UBS, Wachovia, Smith Barney, A.G. Edwards, or some other brokerage firm. Brokers, financial counselors, or whatever title brokerage firms want to call their sales force, ultimately keep or lose their jobs by their own performance in meeting sales targets and bringing in revenue. Brokers don't have to suggest the best investments or asset allocation for their clients. Securities laws only require brokers to sell "suitable" financial and investment products to clients. The problem is that "suitable" does not necessarily mean what's "best" for the client.

Suitability vs. Best Interest

Let's say you have $10,000 a year to save for retirement. A "registered" financial adviser could recommend you invest the money in a low-cost index fund that might net you a return of 8 percent a year. After thirty years, you'd have over $1.1 million. But let's say a broker or so-called "financial counselor" could earn a fat commission for recommending a higher-cost investment being promoted by his financial-services firm. So instead of netting 8 percent a year, you might net 6 percent. After thirty years, your nest egg would grow to just under $800,000, a difference of more than $300,000. The high-cost investment might be perfectly "suitable," since it meets your financial objective of saving for retirement, even though it could leave you significantly poorer than had you invested in the index fund.

While it's admittedly self-serving for me to explain the many reasons why Registered Investment Advisors like Capital Wealth Management are more worthy of your trust than our competitors in the brokerage and insurance industries who also call themselves financial advisors, this is information you need to know to protect your retirement portfolio and your family's financial security. Choosing financial advisers is an important first step toward successful investment planning. Having access to sound, objective financial advice is key to your long-term financial success. With that in mind, you should take the time to choose your financial adviser just as carefully as you would a family doctor or a lawyer.

How Advisors Are Compensated

You've been managing your own retirement savings and have been pretty happy with your investment decisions. However, the task of going it alone is becoming a little overwhelming, so you have decided that it is time to seek the services of a financial professional. The good news is that more advice is available to more investors than ever before. There are many individuals and firms that offer financial advice. The bad news is that with more than sixty-five thousand financial advisers in the United States, looking for professional investment advice can be confusing and frustrating.

Among those calling themselves financial advisors are bankers, lawyers, accountants, insurance agents, stock brokers, and financial planners, to name a few. But how many of these individuals are really interested in providing you financial advice? Which ones are looking out for your best interests as opposed to their own? Which ones would rather sell you products and services? Which ones have a fiduciary responsibility to act in the best interests of their clients? That depends on what type of advisor you hire and on how they shall be compensated by you for their services. In general, a financial advisor gets paid by clients in one of four ways. Below is an overview of these different fee arrangements:

Commission Only

Commission-only advisors receive a percentage of the sales amount on the financial products they recommend, such as mutual funds, stocks, bonds, and insurance. For example, if you invest $10,000 in a 5 percent front-end-load mutual fund, $9,500 is invested in your account and $500 goes to the financial advisor and his firm. Brokers and commission-based advisors, almost always, work for a bank, brokerage firm, or insurance company. A potential conflict of interest with commission-only advisors is that once you make the purchase and the advisor has received the commission, there's really no financial incentive for him or her to continue overseeing your account. Once they get paid for that transaction, commission-only advisors need to move on and find new business.

Fee Only

Fee-only advisors are compensated solely by fees paid by their clients and do not accept commissions or compensation from any other source. They don't get commissions from mutual funds, and they don't sell insurance or other financial products. Unlike commission-based advisors who are compensated up front, fee-only advisors are paid an annual fee to manage their client's assets. As a result, a fee-only investment advisor is a partner in both the potential growth, and possible loss, in a client's portfolio. In other words, if the value of the client's account increases, the investment advisor's fee increases as well. If the client's account value decreases, the investment advisor's fee decreases as well. Less than 1 percent of all financial advisors are true fee-only advisors.

Fee Based

Not to be confused with fee-only advisors, "fee-based" advisors charge fees for advisory services and also receive commissions for selling products. They are typically independent advisors who are affiliated with a broker/dealer as a registered representative and also are a representative of an investment advisor. Typically, a fee is charged for doing a financial plan, and then a commission is charged on any investment products you elect to purchase.

Fee Offset

Under a fee-offset arrangement, a planner imposes a fee for drawing up a strategy, then reduces up to 100 percent of that fee to account for any commissions that may be earned in implementing the plan. The problem of commission bias is less obvious, but it remains. After all, if a financial plan costs $2,000, and the planner earns $10,000 in commissions for selling the needed products, he or she will be able to pocket $8,000 in conflict-producing commissions even after totally offsetting the cost of the original plan.

If you want an advisor whose interests are aligned with yours, it's important to understand, and be comfortable with, the way your financial advisor gets paid—and you need to make sure the advisor's compensation method is suited to your particular needs and situation. So, how can you find out if your current or potential financial advisor is acting in your best interests? Create a form where you list your current or potential advisor's name and firm at the top. Then list these three specific questions below:

1. Are you held to a fiduciary standard in all the services that you provide to me?
2. Do you fully disclose all conflicts of interest that would exist or may potentially exist in our relationship?
3. Do you fully disclose how you are compensated for the services that you render to me in dollar terms, whether directly or from other third parties?

At the bottom, designate a space for signature and date. Present this form to your current or potential advisor and ask them if they would sign this. I think you will find out rather quickly if the financial advisor is working for you or for somebody else.

Notes

Notes

Glossary

advisor: One who gives investment advice for a fee.

asset class: A concentration of securities with similar risk/return characteristics, i.e., size of companies or growth/value tilt.

asset allocation: The placement of a certain percentage of investment capital within different types of assets (e.g., 50 percent in stock, 30 percent in bonds, and 20 percent in cash).

balanced fund: Mutual fund that holds bonds and/or preferred stock in a certain proportion to common stock in order to obtain both current income and long-term growth of principal.

bear market: Term used to describe a prolonged period of declining stock prices.

bond fund: Mutual fund that holds mainly municipal, corporate, and/or government bonds.

broker: A professional who transfers investors' orders to buy and sell securities and generally provides some financial advice.

bull market: Term used to describe a prolonged period of rising stock prices.

capital gains distribution: Payment to investors of profits realized upon the sale of securities.

class A shares: Mutual fund shares that incur a front-end sales charge upon purchase.

class B shares: Mutual fund shares that incur a back-end sales charge (also known as a contingent deferred sales charge or CDSC) if sold within five to six years of purchase.

class C shares: Mutual fund shares that incur higher management and marketing fees than classes A and B, but no sales or redemption charges upon purchase or sale.

diversification: The policy of spreading assets among different investments to reduce the risk of a decline in the overall portfolio.

expense ratio: The percentage of a mutual fund savings taken out of a fund to pay expenses (portfolio management fees, advertising expenses, custody fees).

Federal Reserve: The central bank of the United States, comprised of a twelve-member policy-making board.

fee-only compensation: An arrangement in which a financial advisor charges by an hourly rate, or by an agreed-upon percentage of assets under management, rather than on a trading commission on securities purchases or sales.

fiduciary: An individual, corporation, or association that is charged with managing or investing assets for the benefit of others.

401(k) plan: A retirement savings plan sponsored by for-profit companies that allows an employee to contribute pretax dollars to a company investment vehicle until the employee retires or leaves the company.

growth fund: Mutual fund that invests in stocks exhibiting potential for capital appreciation.

investment policy: A formal statement outlining the broad investment objectives of a plan

load: A commission charged by the sponsor of a mutual fund upon the purchase or sale of shares.

market timing: An investment strategy based on predicting short-term price changes in securities.

mutual fund: An investment company that pools money from shareholders and invests in a variety of securities, including stocks, bonds, and money-market securities.

portfolio manager: Any individual(s) in charge of the investment decisions of a portfolio.

Registered Investment Advisor (RIA): An individual or firm who for a fee, provides investment management or counsel to the investing public. The advisor is registered with the Securities and Exchange Commission and operates in compliance with the Commission's regulations and regulatory review.

risk: Exposure to loss of investment capital (i.e., amount of money invested).

Standard & Poor's 500 Index: An index that is widely replicated by stock index mutual funds. Also known as the S&P 500, it consists of five hundred large U.S. companies.

stock: Security that represents a unit of ownership in a corporation.

transaction fee: A charge assessed by a broker for assisting in the trade of a stock or other security.

Treasury bill: A short-term discounted security issued by the U.S. government with a maturity of one year or less.

Treasury bond: A long-term security issued by the U.S. government with a maturity of ten years or more.

Treasury note: An intermediate-term security issued by the U.S. government having a maturity of one to ten years.

turnover rate: A measurement of trading activity during the past year.

12b-1 fee: A marketing fee levied on mutual-fund shareholders to pay for advertising and distribution costs, as well as broker compensation.

value stock: A stock with a relatively low price compared to its historical earnings and the value of the issuing company's assets.

volatility: The degree of price fluctuation associated with a given investment, interest rate, or market index. The more price fluctuation that is experienced, the greater the volatility.